KID CHEFS

COOKING WITH FRUIT

Rose Miles

Enslow PUBLISHING

Please visit our website, www.enslow.com. For a free color catalog of all our high-quality books,
call toll free 1-800-398-2504 or fax 1-877-980-4454

Published in 2027 by
Enslow Publishing
2544 Clinton Street
Buffalo, NY 14224

Portions of this work were originally authored by Kristen Rajczak and published as Ingredients for a *Healthy Life: Fantastic Fruit Recipes*. All new material in this edition is authored by Rose Miles.

Cataloging-in-Publication Data
Names: Miles, Rose.
Title: Cooking with fruit / Rose Miles.
Description: Buffalo, NY : Enslow Publishing, 2027. | Series: Kid chefs | Includes glossary and index.
Identifiers: ISBN 9781978548541 (pbk.) | ISBN 9781978548558 (library bound) | ISBN 9781978548565 (ebook)
Subjects: LCSH: Cooking (Fruit)--Juvenile literature. | Fruit--Juvenile literature.
Classification: LCC TX811.M674 2027 | DDC 641.34--dc23

Printed in China

Photos Credits: Cover, p. 1 JeniFoto/Shutterstock.com; cover, p. 1 AlenD/Shutterstock.com; cover, p. 1 Sergii Koval/Shutterstock.com; cover, p. 1 Peter Hermes Furian/Shutterstock.com; cover, p. 1 grey_and/Shutterstock.com; p. 4, 6, 8, 10, 12, 14, 16, 18 ricorico/Shutterstock.com; p. 5 spass/Shutterstock.com; p. 6 Sunwand24/Shutterstock.com; p. 7 acceptphoto/Shutterstock.com; p. 8 Diana Taliun/Shutterstock.com; p. 9 Photoongraphy/Shutterstock.com; p. 9 baibaz/Shutterstock.com; p. 9 Photoongraphy/Shutterstock.com; p. 12 MaskaRad/Shutterstock.com; p. 13 Bronwyn Photo/Shutterstock.com; p. 14 Robert Arthur Designs/Shutterstock.com; p. 14 Nikolay132/Shutterstock.com; p. 15 Nitr/Shutterstock.com; p. 16 milsamil/Shutterstock.com; p. 17 JeniFoto/Shutterstock.com; p. 18 Artem Kutsenko/Shutterstock.com; p. 19 AlexeiLogvinovich/Shutterstock.com; p. 20 Nicole Kandi/Shutterstock.com; p. 20 bergamont/Shutterstock.com; p. 21 MillaF/Shutterstock.com; p. 23 ZeiMomArt/Shutterstock.com; p. 10, 11 Markus Mainka/Shutterstock.com

CPSIA compliance information: Batch #QSENS27: For further information, contact Enslow Publishing, New York, New York, at 1-800-398-2504.

Contents

Recipes in this book may use knives, mixers, and hot stove tops. Ask for an adult's help when using these tools.

Words in the glossary appear in **bold** type the first time they are used in the text.

What's Your Favorite Fruit?

Fruit is tasty and healthy—and there's so much to choose from! From juicy watermelon and tart cranberries to crisp apples and sweet peaches, fruit comes in many shapes, sizes, and flavors.

Grabbing a piece of fresh fruit to snack on is always a good idea. But did you know that there are tons of **recipes** you can make to include even more fruit in your **diet**? Keep reading to learn some awesome ways to eat fruit every day. You may just find your new favorite!

Do You Have Allergies?

The recipes in this book may use **ingredients** that contain or have come into contact with nuts, gluten, dairy products, and other common causes of **allergies**. If you have any food allergies, please ask a parent or teacher for help when cooking and tasting!

Many fruit-flavored foods don't actually have any fruit in them. Fresh fruit is best!

Where Do Fruits Come From?

Fruits come from the flower of a plant. The fruit holds the seeds of the plants it grew from. The job of the fruit is to spread the seeds to grow more plants!

Some fruits, like cherries, are called stone fruits. These have one big seed, or pit, at their center. Oranges, on the other hand, have seeds throughout their flesh.

Some fruits, such as cucumbers, tomatoes, and squash, are often mistaken for vegetables because of their taste. But they are fruits—the seeds are on the inside!

Tasty Tidbits

It seems strange, based on the definition of a fruit, but farmers have found ways to grow some fruits without seeds. Today, seedless oranges and watermelon are common.

Fruits come in every color you can imagine!

Fresh or Frozen Fruit?

You can buy fresh fruit from the produce aisle, or frozen fruit from the freezer aisle. But which is better? That depends on how you're eating it!

Many people think fresh fruit tastes better and has a better texture. That makes it great for snacking.

Frozen fruits are convenient and will last much longer without spoiling. They're great for smoothies, baking, and cooking. And don't worry—the fruits are frozen when they're at their ripest. Frozen fruit is just as healthy as fresh fruit.

Tasty Tidbits

Dried cherries, plums, and apricots are also very tasty. Try to keep your serving size small because these have a lot of sugar in them.

Fruity Smoothie

makes 2 big servings or 4 smaller servings

Ingredients:

1 cup frozen cherries

1 cup frozen pineapple

½ frozen banana (peel before freezing)

1 cup orange juice

½ cup low-fat yogurt

Directions:

1. Mix the orange juice and yogurt in a blender.
2. Add the frozen fruit. Blend until smooth. If your blender has trouble mixing them all or the smoothie looks too thick, add another ½ cup of orange juice or water.
3. Serve immediately or store covered in the fridge. The smoothie will keep for about a day and just needs a quick stir.

Mix it up! You can swap out the fruit in this recipe for others, such as blueberries, strawberries, or blackberries. Try lots of different options to find your favorite!

Super Superfoods

Fruits are considered **superfoods** because they're packed with **nutrients** that help keep you healthy. Eating fruit may help stop you from getting certain diseases, such as cancer and heart disease. It also aids in keeping a healthy weight.

All fruits are good for you, but they are good in different ways. Different fruits offer different nutrients. It's smart—and tasty—to eat fruits of many colors!

A good thing to keep in mind is "eating the rainbow." This means eating fruits of different colors every day. From red strawberries to yellow bananas to blueberries, the possibilities are endless (and colorful)!

Tasty Tidbits

No one knows exactly how many types of fruit there are in the world. Some people say there may be as many as 20,000!

Fruits are packed with many health benefits. Check out this list of nutrients your body needs and the fruits that provide them!

NUTRIENT	WHAT IT DOES	WHAT TO EAT
vitamin C	**protects** the body and **cells** from disease and damage	strawberries, oranges, kiwifruits, cranberries, limes
vitamin A	maintains eye health; aids in cell growth; helps the heart, lungs, and kidneys work correctly	apricots, cantaloupes, grapefruits, watermelons
folic acid	helps the body make red blood cells and skin cells; aids in strengthening bones; keeps nerves working well	strawberries, bananas, melons, lemons, pineapples
potassium	maintains normal blood pressure; keeps kidneys working correctly	papayas, cantaloupes, dried plums, oranges, kiwifruits
magnesium	maintains muscle and nerve activities; aids in strengthening bones; helps keep blood sugar levels and blood pressure normal	bananas, raisins, raspberries, watermelons

An Apple a Day

When Europeans settled the Americas, they brought juicy apples with them. Today, apples are grown across North America, but the Pacific Northwest is known for growing especially beautiful fruits.

The old saying "an apple a day keeps the doctor away" may be true! Apples are a good source of fiber and vitamins A and C, as well as substances called **antioxidants**. Scientists believe these compounds help the body fight disease and repair itself.

Tasty Tidbits

There are thousands of kinds of apples. They fall into three general groups: cider apples, cooking apples, and dessert apples.

Amazing Apple Pie

Makes about 8 servings

Ingredients:

10 cups peeled and thinly sliced Granny Smith apples (about 3 pounds)
¾ cup sugar
1 ½ tablespoons flour
1 teaspoon ground cinnamon
½ teaspoon salt
¼ teaspoon ground nutmeg
1 tablespoon chilled butter, cut into small pieces
2 9-inch prepared piecrusts

If you'd like to make your own piecrust, there are lots of recipes online—or a family member might have one!

Directions:

1. Preheat oven to 425 degrees.
2. Mix apples with sugar, flour, cinnamon, salt, and nutmeg.
3. Lightly spray a 9-inch pie pan with cooking spray. Lay one of the prepared piecrusts in the pan, gently fitting it to the sides and bottom.
4. Spoon the apple filling into the piecrust. Sprinkle the small pieces of butter over the top.
5. Place the second piecrust over the filling. Use your fingers to pinch the edges of the top crust and bottom crust together.
6. Cut a few slits in the top crust to let steam escape.
7. Place the pie on a baking sheet and bake for 10 minutes. Lower the oven temperature to 350 degrees and bake for another 40 minutes. Allow the pie to cool before cutting.

Summertime Strawberries

California produces about 90 percent of the strawberries that are grown in the United States. Now, these beautiful berries are grown all over the world.

Aside from giving us lots of beneficial **vitamins** and **minerals**, strawberries are very useful in the kitchen. They can be eaten fresh, perhaps sliced on cereal or yogurt. They can be baked into pies and breads. Strawberries are fairly easy to turn into a delicious jam and can even be made into sweet, cold soup! Strawberries aren't just tasty—they're good for you too!

Tasty Tidbits

Strawberries are the only fruit with seeds on the outside. There are about 200 seeds on each berry.

Strawberry Salad

makes 2 servings

Ingredients:

Dressing:

4 tablespoons balsamic vinegar
2 tablespoons extra-virgin olive oil
a pinch of salt and pepper

Salad:

1 cup sliced strawberries
¼ cup very thinly sliced red onion
3 cups baby spinach, washed and dried
¼ cup chopped walnuts, almonds, or pecans
¼ cup crumbled feta cheese

You can even add some grilled chicken on top of this healthy salad for some extra protein.

Directions:

1. To make the dressing, measure the balsamic vinegar and extra-virgin olive oil into a jar with a lid. Add the salt and pepper. Put the lid on the jar and shake it up.
2. Place your spinach in a big mixing bowl. Pour the dressing over the top and toss to coat the leaves.
3. Divide the spinach between two plates. Add half of the strawberries, onion, nuts, and cheese to each.

Sweet Citrus

There's nothing like an ice-cold lemonade on a hot summer day. Lemons, along with limes, grapefruits, and oranges, are citrus fruits. They are among some of the most popular flavors used in the United States. These fruits are full of folic acid, potassium, and of course, vitamin C!

There are so many ways to use the juices of citrus fruits in both sweet and savory foods. Think of the cool, refreshing tastes of key lime pie, orange sherbet, and lemon ice. Or you can mix them with olive oil for a tasty salad dressing.

Tasty Tidbits

Fruit juices can count toward your servings of fruit every day. Be sure you are drinking 100 percent fruit juice, which can give you important vitamins and minerals. Don't forget to eat whole fruit for its fiber too.

Homemade Lemonade

makes 6 servings

Ingredients:

1 cup freshly squeezed lemon juice (from about 6 lemons)

4 cups cold water, plus 1 cup

½ cup honey

It takes a bit of work to squeeze those lemons, but the taste of freshly made lemonade is worth it!

Directions:

1. Pour 1 cup water into a small pan on the stovetop. Add honey. Stir while it heats and comes to a boil.
2. Pour the water and honey mixture into a pitcher.
3. Stir in the 4 cups of cold water and lemon juice.
4. Chill in the fridge for about 2 hours.

Around the World

You can probably find apples, bananas, grapes, and oranges at your local grocery store. But so many more types of fruit are found and enjoyed around the world!

Durian can be found in Southeast Asia. It has a spiky outside and creamy inside. It is famous for its strong odor!

Lychee is found in China and India. The inside feels a little like a grape. It has a sweet and floral taste.

Also native to China, kumquat kind of looks like an orange, but it is much smaller—about the size of an olive!

Tasty Tidbits

Did you know the avocado is a fruit too? That big pit on the inside is the seed! Avocados are grown in Florida and California, but Mexico provides more than half of the avocados sold in the United States.

Fun Fruit Pizza

Ingredients:

Makes 6 big servings

Crust:

1 cup all-purpose flour
1 cup whole-wheat flour
½ cup sugar
1 teaspoon baking powder
½ cup (1 stick) of butter, plus 2 tablespoons
2 eggs
1 teaspoon vanilla extract

Topping:

1 ½ cups vanilla Greek yogurt
fruit (sliced strawberries, blueberries, kiwifruit, pineapple, or your favorite)

Who knew that you could have pizza for dessert? This cool recipe makes a fun and tasty treat.

Directions:

1. Use a food processor to mix the flours, sugar, baking powder, and butter until it looks crumb-like.
2. In a separate bowl, whisk together the eggs and vanilla. Pour this into the food processor and mix until a lump of slightly crumbly dough forms.
3. Press the dough evenly onto a greased pan or cookie sheet. Bake for 6 to 8 minutes.
4. Let the crust cool. Then, spread the yogurt onto the cooled crust. Arrange the fruit on top. Cut into slices and enjoy!

Mix It Up

Scientists have found ways to cross fruit plants to make new fruits. Have you ever heard of a pluot? It is a cross between a plum and an apricot! Some people like these **hybrids**. Others think their names, like tangelo (a tangerine crossed with a pomelo or grapefruit), just sound silly.

Whatever side you're on, fruits are some of the healthiest snacks around. Grab a pluot for a tasty treat that will give you the nutrients your body needs!

Why Eat Fruit?

Fruits Fill You Up

- Fruits are a great source of fiber. Because fiber makes us feel full, eating fruit can stop us from eating too much junk food!

Fruits Boost Immunity

- No one likes having a cold! Some fruits are packed with vitamin C, which helps fight off colds.

Fruits are Hydrating

- Fruits like melons, grapes, and oranges have lots of water. Drinking enough water is super important for doing well in sports, thinking clearly, and staying healthy.

Fruits Make You Feel Good

- Making healthy food choices often lead to more and more healthy choices!

Glossary

allergy: a body's sensitivity to usually harmless things in the surroundings, such as dust, pollen, or mold

antioxidants: special molecules that help protect our bodies from harmful things; they keep our cells healthy

cell: the smallest basic part of a living thing

diet: the food one usually eats

hybrid: the offspring of two animals or plants of different kinds

ingredient: a food that is mixed with other foods

mineral: a substance important in small quantities for the nutrition of animals

nutrient: something a living thing needs to grow and stay alive

protect: to keep safe

recipe: an explanation of how to make food

superfoods: foods that are super healthy because they are rich in antioxidants, vitamins, and minerals

vitamin: a substance important in small quantities for the nutrition of animals

Fact Check

1. What fruit is a great source of vitamin C?
   a. apples
   b. pineapples
   c. bananas

2. What fruit is famous for its odor?
   a. durians
   b. kiwifruits
   c. raisins

3. A pluot is a cross between a ________ and an apricot.
   a. peach
   b. pear
   c. plum

Answers: 1. a, 2. a, 3. c

On the Internet

Fruit
www.freshforkids.com.au/fruit
Check out Fresh for Kids to learn all you need to know about lots of different fruits!

Recipes
www.superhealthykids.com/healthy-kids-recipes.php
Check out this list of healthy, yummy recipes for all your meals!

Publisher's note to educators and parents: Our editors have carefully reviewed these websites to ensure that they are suitable for students. Many websites change frequently, however, and we cannot guarantee that a site's future contents will continue to meet our high standards of quality and educational value. Be advised that students should be closely supervised whenever they access the Internet.

Index